# STONEHENGE AND AVEBURY

## AND NEIGHBOURING MONUMENTS

**AN ILLUSTRATED GUIDE**

Text by R. J. C. Atkinson
*Professor of Archaeology, University College, Cardiff*

Cover picture and reconstruction drawings by Alan Sorrell

Maps and plans by Reitz

Her Majesty's Stationery Office, London 1959

# HOW TO USE THIS GUIDE BOOK

This booklet is published as a guide for visitors to the most famous groups of prehistoric monuments in Britain, around Stonehenge and Avebury. The Stonehenge area is described on pages 12–37, and the Avebury district on pages 38–55. The builders of these sites, and the methods they used, are discussed at the beginning and end (pages 4–11, 56–63).

The dates given are based on the radiocarbon process, which uses the natural radioactivity of plant and animal remains to estimate their age. They must be treated as very rough guides only.

The map on this page shows how to reach Stonehenge and Avebury, and there are more detailed maps of the two districts on the back cover.

The drawings by Alan Sorrell give an idea of what the people and their monuments *may* have looked like in the past; but they must not be taken as authentic reconstructions, since in most cases there is not enough evidence for certainty.

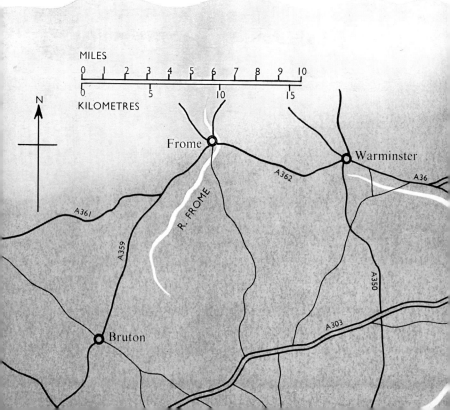

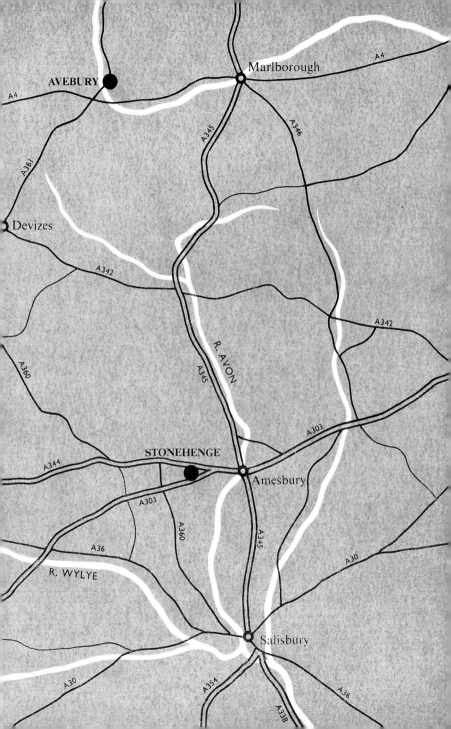

# The People and the Monuments

All the monuments described in this guide belong to the Neolithic period (or New Stone Age) and to the earlier part of the Bronze Age; or, in round figures, between 3000 and 1200 BC. Apart from the causewayed camps like Windmill Hill (page 54) they are all connected either with religious practices or with the burial of the dead. None of the houses of their builders survives, probably because in the course of the last three or four thousand years all traces of them have been destroyed by the weathering of the soft chalk rock of the district. Nevertheless, from the study of the monuments themselves and of objects found in them, archaeologists have been able to identify several separate communities which occupied Wiltshire during this period, each with its own traditions, and each responsible for building some of the monuments described.

For many thousands of years, up to about 3000 BC, the population of the region consisted of scattered bands of roving hunters, living on wild game and wild plants. They grew no crops, had no domesticated animals and have left behind them nothing but a few examples of their simple stone tools and flint weapons.

About 3000 BC southern England was colonised for the first time by farming peoples, who brought with them from the Continent the arts of growing grain and breeding cattle. They settled on the chalk downs of

*Some typical possessions of the Windmill Hill people*

*Secondary Neolithic tools, weapons and pottery*

Wessex, leading a simple and apparently peaceful existence in which cattle-herding was supplemented by the hunting of small game and by the cultivation of a primitive form of wheat on scattered patches of ground, cleared of scrub and tilled with stone hoes and wooden digging-sticks. None of their houses survives for certain in Wiltshire; but elsewhere they seem to have been rectangular log-cabins large enough for a single family only. Their tools and weapons were made of flint, bone and antler, and their clothes were probably of leather. Their round-bottomed baggy pots look like imitations of the kind of leather vessels that would be appropriate for a pastoral people.

These earliest farming colonists are known as the Primary Neolithic people, and they built the causewayed camps, like Windmill Hill, the earthen Long Barrows, and the Cursus monuments like the one near Stonehenge.

Some centuries afterwards, but probably not later than 2700 BC, further small groups of settlers crossed from France to south-western England, landing mainly on both shores of the Bristol Channel. These new arrivals brought with them the practice of burying their dead in stone-built tombs under long mounds or cairns; but apart from the tombs themselves they have left no traces, and none of their settlements has been identified. Probably they were few in number and were quickly absorbed by the Primary Neolithic people; for most of the pottery and other objects found in the tombs have been of that type.

The tombs themselves are widely distributed in South Wales and on the Cotswolds, with a small but important group in the region around Avebury. The West Kennet Long Barrow is the largest, and probably one of the earliest, of these tombs in Britain; and there can be little doubt that its builders first introduced into Wiltshire the techniques of building with large stones, which were later to be copied by other peoples, on an even larger scale, at Avebury and Stonehenge.

For some time these early immigrants seem to have lived alongside the remnants of the native hunting peoples, without much contact between them, much in the same way that the aboriginal populations of north America and Australia continued to flourish side by side with European settlers. But in time gradual mixing of the native hunters with the immigrant farmers led to the emergence of new and distinct communities, in which the old traditions of hunting and gathering were supplemented by a number of new skills and techniques which were borrowed from the primary colonists, such as stock-breeding, simple agriculture and the making of pottery.

These new communities are known to archaeologists as the Secondary Neolithic peoples. They seem to have been largely nomadic, and no houses are known, though what may have been camping sites have been found between Avebury and West Kennet and on the downs near Stonehenge. They were clearly skilful workers in wood, since it was they who built the roofed temples at the Sanctuary and Woodhenge; and it is these same people who seem to have invented the large open-air sanctuaries, of which Stonehenge I is the finest and the best known.

About 2000 BC the peaceful peasant life of southern England was startled and disturbed by the arrival of bands of immigrants from Holland and the Rhineland, known as the Beaker people from the common occurrence of pottery drinking-vessels in their graves. Though relatively few in numbers,

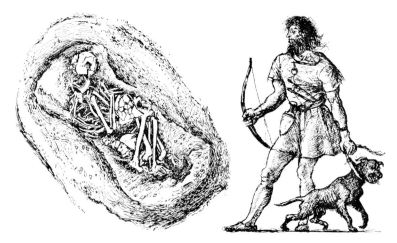

*A Late Neolithic Beaker grave and a Beaker warrior*

*A Wessex chieftain and an Early Bronze Age burial*

they seem to have established themselves as masters over the native population, perhaps in part through their possession of the earliest objects of metal, in copper and gold, to have been found in Britain. The main source of these metals lay in Ireland, and one of the Beaker people's chief activities appears to have been the opening up of trade routes between their main areas of settlement, in eastern Britain, and the sources of supply of these precious metals in the west. One of these routes certainly followed the south coast of Wales and probably accounts for the Beaker traders' familiarity with the Pembrokeshire bluestones which they selected for use at Stonehenge.

The dominant position of the Beaker folk found its expression in the building of a number of great stone circles in Wiltshire, using techniques already introduced by the builders of the West Kennet tomb, and obviously requiring the employment of large bodies of strictly controlled labour. These monuments include the inner circles and Avenue at Avebury, and the double circles at the Sanctuary and Stonehenge II. A little later other groups of Beaker people, reinforced by a second immigration of warriors from northern Europe, seem to have adopted the embanked type of sanctuary of the Secondary Neolithic peoples (such as Stonehenge I and Woodhenge), and to have copied it with certain differences and on an even larger scale. The finest of these Beaker sanctuaries are represented by the great earthworks of the reconstructed Avebury (Avebury II) and Durrington Walls, a ruined site near Woodhenge.

The stones of Stonehenge as they may have

*appeared after the final rebuilding about 1300 BC*

By the time of the Beaker invasions the Primary Neolithic peoples were already beginning to lose their identity and to be absorbed by the Secondary Neolithic communities. For a time these continued to flourish, even though dominated to some extent by the Beaker invaders. But within a century or two the same kind of contact and fusion took place as before, with the emergence of a new and distinctive community in which Beaker and native traditions of life were blended.

To this new community belong the Wessex people of the Early Bronze Age, who owed their great power and wealth, expressed in the rich furnishing of their barrow-burials clustered round Stonehenge and Avebury, to their part in the metal trade between Ireland and the Continent in the years between 1600 and 1300 BC. This widespread and profitable trade extended as far as central Europe and Scandinavia, and to the urban civilisations of Crete and Greece. As a result, Britain became for a time more truly a part of Europe than at any later period, until its incorporation in the Roman empire more than a thousand years afterwards. It is against this background of a rich commercial aristocracy, dominated by a dynasty of commanding chieftains, that we must see the building of Stonehenge III.

In this unique building the very size of the stones, and the labour of their transport and erection, imply the strict control of a very large proportion of the local population over a long period of time; and the fusion in its design of the native traditions of the stone circle and the jointed timber building, with the added refinements of contemporary Mediterranean architecture, symbolises the cultural solidarity and the far-reaching commercial influence of this Golden Age of British prehistory.

The following table shows the relationships and development of the various prehistoric communities described above, and the approximate periods at which their monuments were built. The dates, like all dates in prehistory, must be treated as rough guides only.

*The objects found in the excavations at Woodhenge and from the many local barrows explored in the nineteenth century can be seen in the Museum of the Wiltshire Archaeological Society in Long Street, Devizes. The finds from Stonehenge and from some of the more recent barrow-excavations in the neighbourhood are in the South Wiltshire and Blackmore Museum, St Ann Street, Salisbury*

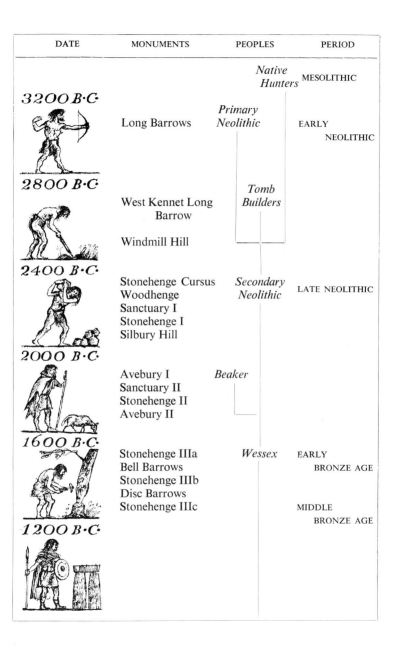

| DATE | MONUMENTS | PEOPLES | PERIOD |
|---|---|---|---|
| | | *Native Hunters* | MESOLITHIC |
| 3200 B·C | Long Barrows | *Primary Neolithic* | EARLY NEOLITHIC |
| 2800 B·C | West Kennet Long Barrow | *Tomb Builders* | |
| | Windmill Hill | | |
| 2400 B·C | Stonehenge Cursus Woodhenge Sanctuary I Stonehenge I Silbury Hill | *Secondary Neolithic* | LATE NEOLITHIC |
| 2000 B·C | Avebury I Sanctuary II Stonehenge II Avebury II | *Beaker* | |
| 1600 B·C | Stonehenge IIIa Bell Barrows Stonehenge IIIb Disc Barrows Stonehenge IIIc | *Wessex* | EARLY BRONZE AGE |
| | | | MIDDLE BRONZE AGE |
| 1200 B·C | | | |

*This aerial view of Stonehenge, seen from the north-north-east, shows the earthwork and the Aubrey Holes just inside it. The beginning of the Avenue can be seen in the foreground to the left*

# Stonehenge

Stonehenge is unique. There is nothing like it anywhere else, and from the earliest times it has aroused the awe and curiosity of its visitors. It was first mentioned, as one of the wonders of Britain, only seventy years after the Norman Conquest; and since then at one time or another almost every people of antiquity has been claimed as its builders.

It is only during the present century that planned archaeological excavations on the site have begun to yield some reliable information about its history and origin. As the result of this work, which has been carried on at intervals since 1901, and culminated in the restoration of some of the fallen stones in 1958–64, it is now possible to say what the main features of Stonehenge are, and roughly when and in what order they were built.

The outer boundary of Stonehenge is the low *bank* which lies about 100 ft (30 m) outside the stones. Originally it stood about 6 ft (2 m) high and was built of chalk rubble quarried from the *ditch* immediately outside it. In the course of centuries most of it has slipped back, obscuring the very irregular outlines of the ditch, which originally consisted simply of a number of rough quarry-pits strung together. One half of the circuit of the ditch was excavated in 1919–26, and was only partly refilled.

The earthwork is broken by a broad *entrance-gap* on the north-east side, and by various smaller gaps elsewhere, some of which are modern. From the entrance the *Avenue*, bounded by a small bank and ditch on either side, runs downhill across the main road and eventually leads to the bank of the River Avon at West Amesbury, about two miles away. Within the Avenue, close to the road, stands the *Heel Stone*, with traces of a circular ditch surrounding its base.

Just inside the bank is a ring of 56 pits, now filled up, which are known as the *Aubrey Holes* after their discoverer John Aubrey (1626–97). About half of them have been excavated and are marked by patches of white chalk on the surface.

At the entrance of the earthwork is a large fallen stone, known as the *Slaughter Stone*. It originally stood upright on its outer end, and together with a similar stone, now vanished, formed a ceremonial doorway to the site. Further round the earthwork, on the line of the Aubrey Holes, are two smaller stones known as the *Station Stones*; and two similar stones, now vanished, also stood within the bank on the north and south sides, each surrounded by a small circular ditch.

The standing stones in the centre consist of two main kinds of rock. The larger blocks and their lintels, as well as the Station Stones, Slaughter Stone and Heel Stone, are all of *sarsen*, a kind of natural sandstone which occurs as huge boulders on the surface of the Marlborough Downs, about

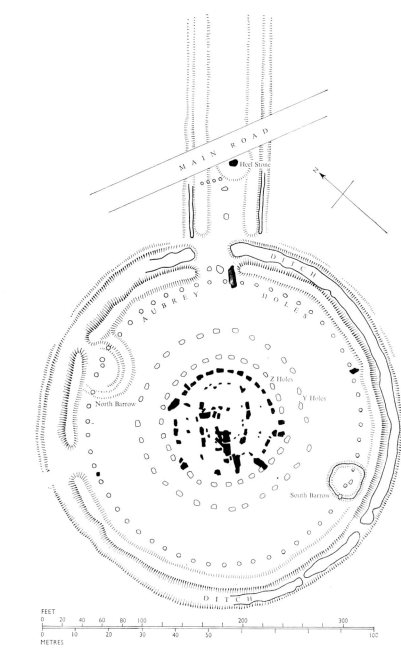

MAIN ROAD

Heel Stone

N

DITCH

AUBREY HOLES

Z Holes

Y Holes

North Barrow

South Barrow

DITCH

FEET
0　20　40　60　80　100　　　　　　200　　　　　　　300
0　　10　　20　　30　　40　　50　　　　　　　　　　　100
METRES

*Plan of Stonehenge. The stones are marked in black*

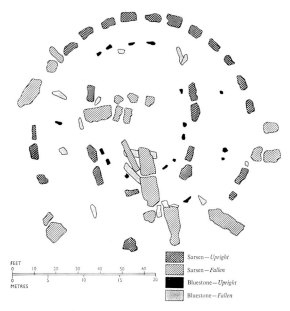

FEET

| 0 | 10 | 20 | 30 | 40 | 50 | 60 |

| 0 | 5 | 10 | 15 | 20 |

METRES

■ Sarsen—*Upright*

▨ Sarsen—*Fallen*

■ Bluestone—*Upright*

▨ Bluestone—*Fallen*

*Plan of the stones as they are today*

20 miles north of Stonehenge. The smaller stones, known as the *Bluestones*, are of several kinds of blue-coloured rock which were fetched by the builders from the Prescelly Mountains in south-west Wales.

The *Sarsen Circle*, about 100 ft (30 m) in diameter, consisted originally of 30 uprights, each weighing about 25 tons, capped by a continuous ring of 30 lintels weighing about 7 tons. Inside it was a horseshoe of five *Sarsen Trilithons*, each trilithon consisting of a pair of huge uprights, weighing up to 45 tons, capped by a massive lintel.

Apart from the Heel Stone and the eastern Station Stone, all the sarsens have been carefully dressed to shape by pounding their surfaces with stone hammers. The uprights are slightly 'dished' on the top to provide a secure seating for the lintels, and projecting tenons worked on them fit into corresponding hollow mortice-holes on the undersides of the lintels. In addition, the lintels of the outer circle are fitted to each other with tongue-and-groove joints.

The *Bluestone Circle*, now much ruined and incomplete, stands inside the sarsen circle. Originally it consisted of about 60 stones, set close together. Only two of the surviving stones have been dressed to shape. Both of them had formerly been used as lintel-stones.

PERIOD I
about 2200 BC

# THE HISTORY

## OF

## STONEHENGE

PERIOD IIIa
about 1600 BC

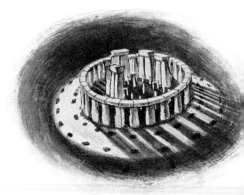

PERIOD IIIb
1550–1400 BC

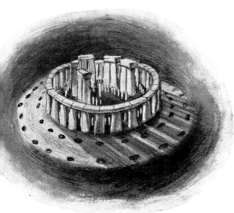

PERIOD IIIc
about 1300 BC

*These drawings show the stages in the development of Stonehenge. In Period I there were only three stones, near the entrance. In Period II the double circle of bluestones and the Avenue were added. The sarsen stones replaced them in Period IIIa, and in Period IIIb some bluestones were erected in the centre, and the Y and Z Holes were dug. In the last Period, IIIc, the bluestones were re-arranged as they are today*

The *Bluestone Horseshoe* stands inside the sarsen horseshoe and originally had 19 stones, which increased in height towards the centre. All of them have been dressed to shape, and two bear traces on their tops of projecting tenons, which have been almost battered away. Another has a dished top, like the sarsen uprights, and the adjacent upright has a groove worked all down one side. This stone must once have fitted another with a corresponding tongue, which now survives only as a stump below the surface.

At the focus of the bluestone horseshoe is the *Altar Stone*, a dressed block of sandstone from the shores of Milford Haven in Pembrokeshire, about 16 ft (5 m) long. It is now buried in the ground beneath the fallen stones of the great sarsen trilithon, but it probably stood upright as a pillar originally.

In addition to these visible features, two settings of pits were discovered during excavations and are not marked on the surface. The *Y and Z Holes* lie about 36 ft (11 m) and 12 ft (3·7 m) respectively outside the sarsen circle. There are 30 pits in the Y ring and only 29 in the Z ring. One Z hole on the west side lies beneath a fallen sarsen, and another to the south-east is missing altogether. The *Q and R Holes* form the ends of a series of dumb-bell-shaped trenches, arranged radially, which lie beneath the line of the present bluestone circle. They originally held the bluestones in two concentric circles about 6 ft (2 m) apart.

# The History of Stonehenge

As in many of our later cathedrals and churches, not all the structures we see at Stonehenge today were built at the same time. As a result of the recent excavations, we can now divide the history of Stonehenge into three main periods, covering a span of about nine centuries, between 2200 and 1300 BC.

**Period I** The earliest structures were the bank and ditch, the Heel Stone, and the Aubrey Holes. There was probably some kind of wooden gateway or ceremonial arch a little to the west of the Heel Stone, and a pair of small stones in the entrance of the earthwork forming a kind of door. Perhaps, too, there was some small building, or a setting of stones, in the unexcavated area at the very centre. The Aubrey Holes never held any kind of wooden or stone upright, and though many of the excavated holes were found to contain cremated human bones, they do not seem to have been intended as graves. They were probably dug as part of some religious ceremony.

Similar open-air sanctuaries, though of smaller size, containing a ring of pits with cremated burials, have been discovered near Oxford and near

*The Heel Stone seen from the west*

Above: *The entrance to the outer circle of sarsen stones is beneath the middle lintel.* Below: *The first sarsen trilithon, with two pillars of the bluestone horseshoe to the right*

Linlithgow in Scotland. All of them, including Stonehenge I, seem to belong to the Late Neolithic period, about 2000 BC. Unfortunately, apart from the digging of pits, nothing is known about the ceremonies for which they were used.

**Period II** About 500 years later than the building of the first Stonehenge, the monument was radically remodelled. At least 80 bluestones, weighing up to four tons apiece, were brought from the Prescelly Mountains in Pembrokeshire and from the shores of Milford Haven in the same county, and were set up in the Q and R Holes, forming a double circle in the centre of the site. This circle had an entrance on the north-east side, marked by additional stones on the inside, and on the opposite side was a large pit, which may have held a stone of exceptional size, such as the present Altar Stone.

The axis of this circle, from the pit through the entrance, pointed towards the sunrise at the summer solstice, on the longest day of the year. In order to make the entrance of the older earthwork fit this new axis, about 25 ft (7·6 m) of the bank on the east side of the entrance gap was thrown back into the ditch, to widen the original causeway. At the same time the Avenue was made, leading up to this entrance from the bank of the River Avon. It probably marks the route by which the bluestones were hauled up to the site. The new Avenue enclosed the Heel Stone, which was now given a kind of symbolic protection by digging a ditch around it; this was almost at once filled up again.

This first bluestone circle at Stonehenge was probably the work of the Beaker people, who colonised Britain from the Continent at the end of the Neolithic period and may possibly have introduced the idea of sky- or sun-worship. The excavations have shown in fact that they never completed their work at Stonehenge, since there is a gap in the circle, of unknown extent, on the west side, and two of the flanking stones at the entrance were never set up, though the holes for them had been partially dug. The date of this circle is probably between 1700 and 1600 BC.

**Period IIIa** Not long after 1600 BC, the rising power and wealth of the Early Bronze Age inhabitants of Wessex found its expression in an even more radical reconstruction of Stonehenge.

The double circle of bluestones, still unfinished, was dismantled and its stones put on one side. In their place over 80 enormous blocks of sarsen stone were dragged from the Marlborough Downs and set up in the lintelled circle and horseshoe of trilithons which we see today, together with the four Station Stones and the gateway formed by the Slaughter Stone and its vanished companion. The axis of this new monument, like that of the circle it replaced, points towards the midsummer sunrise.

This extraordinary building exhibits a number of refinements which do not occur anywhere else among the stone monuments of prehistoric Europe. The squaring and dressing of the stones, their joints and the elaborate shaping of the lintels, as well as the high degree of accuracy achieved in placing the stones, all point to influence from the urban civilisations of Minoan Crete and Mycenean Greece, in which alone at this time was any sophisticated architecture to be found.

Connections between Britain and the Mediterranean at this period had already been suspected, from the finding in British barrow-burials, some of them close to Stonehenge, of objects imported or copied from Mediterranean sources. In 1953 these connections were dramatically confirmed by the discovery at Stonehenge of carvings of bronze axeheads and a bronze dagger. The axes are all of a type which was made in Ireland and exported to the Continent between 1600 and 1400 BC; but the best match for the dagger comes from the Shaft Graves of Mycenae in southern Greece, the legendary home of Agamemnon.

From this and other evidence the erection of the sarsen stones at Stonehenge can be dated soon after 1600 BC. The architect (for surely the designer of such a building deserves the title) must almost certainly have been a man who was familiar with the buildings of the contemporary urban civilisations of the Mediterranean world.

**Period IIIb** Soon after the sarsen stones had been set up, and perhaps as part of the same design, rather more than twenty of the dismantled bluestones were selected, carefully dressed to shape, and erected in an oval setting on the line of the present bluestone horseshoe. Only a few of the stone-holes for this setting have so far been identified, so that its exact plan is still uncertain. But it is clear that it included at least two miniature copies of the great sarsen trilithons, of which the lintels and some of the uprights with traces of tenons still survive, though re-used in a different way. The tongued and grooved bluestones, and the present Altar Stone, must have formed part of this oval setting.

It seems clear that to complete the monument the builders intended to use the remaining 60 bluestones, which had not so far been dressed to shape; and it is almost certainly to hold these that the two rings of Y and Z Holes were dug. But for some reason, perhaps an unforeseen catastrophe or an unlucky omen, this project was abandoned unfinished. The last few holes to be dug, on the east side, were irregular and incomplete, and no stones were ever set up in any of them. Instead, the whole design was given up, and the oval setting of dressed bluestones in the centre was demolished.

**Period IIIc** The final reconstruction of Stonehenge probably followed almost at once. The uprights of the dressed oval structure were re-set in the horseshoe of bluestones we see today, with the tenons of the miniature

Above: *The bluestone circle is best preserved just within the entrance*

Below: *Carvings of a bronze dagger and bronze axe-heads were found in 1953*
*The drawing on the right shows them in greater detail*

Stonehenge has aroused the interest of painters and engravers since before AD 1600. The upper engraving was made by David Loggan towards the end of the seventeenth century, and shows the upright of the central trilithon leaning towards the centre. It was straightened in 1901. The leaning stone on the far right is now lying almost flat. The view below, about a century later, is typical of the romantic approach to prehistoric monuments which developed during the eighteenth century

Above: *The mortice and tenon joints are best seen on the tallest stone and its fallen lintel.* Below: *The tenon on the tallest stone is nine inches high*

trilithons battered down and almost obliterated. The two lintels were set up as pillars in the bluestone circle, with their mortices facing outwards so that they could not be seen from the centre. Both of them have since fallen over in different directions, so that the mortices on one of them now lie underground.

The rest of the circle was made up of the undressed bluestones which had earlier been intended for the Y and Z Holes. Originally the total number of stones in this circle must have been at least 60, set quite close together, but most of them have since disappeared.

The largest bluestone of all, the Altar Stone, was probably set up as a tall pillar in front of the central sarsen trilithon and has since fallen down.

The date of this final reconstruction is probably around 1300 BC, during the Middle Bronze Age.

Since that date the history of the site is one of damage and destruction. Many stones are now missing altogether, and others survive only as stumps below ground level; while the soil, which extends as far as the car-park, is filled with fragments of the stones which have been broken up. Much of this destruction is certainly due to visitors, who delighted in knocking off fragments as keepsakes. Indeed, at one time a hammer could regularly be hired in Amesbury for this very purpose. One must remember, too, that there is no natural building-stone available in the neighbourhood so that from the Middle Ages onwards Stonehenge must have provided a convenient quarry for local builders. It is known, too, that up to about a century ago the local farmers used regularly to break up the smaller stones for road metal, to repair farm tracks. Many of the bluestones have probably disappeared in this way.

It has long been recognised that the axis of Stonehenge III points to the midsummer sunrise and, in the opposite direction, to the midwinter sunset; and it is now known that this alignment goes back to period II, if not earlier. Recently it has been claimed that Stonehenge incorporates other significant astronomical alignments, and that it was used to predict eclipses of the sun and moon.

Some of these claims are so extravagant that they cannot be taken seriously, and none of them is easy to verify, because the ruined state of Stonehenge makes it almost impossible to recover, with sufficient accuracy, the original direction of any supposed alignment. None the less, it does seem likely that lines drawn between the Station Stones (including the diagonal joining the two surviving stones) marked the directions of the rising and settings of the sun and moon at midsummer and midwinter. If so, these alignments must have been established in period I, since the diagonal line of sight would have been blocked by the stone circles of periods II and III. The Station Stones may thus perpetuate the sites of an earlier set of markers, possibly of timber.

## THE DRUIDS

Ever since it was first suggested, three hundred years ago, that stone circles were Druidical temples, it has been popularly supposed that Stonehenge was built and used by the Druids. Unfortunately there is no foundation for this belief at all. The Druids were a Celtic priesthood which flourished in Britain only during the few centuries before the Roman Conquest. It is very unlikely that there were any Druids in these islands before 250 BC, and by that time Stonehenge had been built for more than a thousand years and may already have been partly in ruins.

The names given to two of the stones, the Altar Stone and the Slaughter Stone, are popularly connected with the idea of human sacrifice. But they were invented, by over-imaginative antiquaries, only during the last three centuries, and there is no evidence at all for supposing that human sacrifice was practised at Stonehenge at any time during its long history.

# The Avenue

The Stonehenge Avenue (picture on page 35) provides a formal approach to the monument, and links it by an indirect route to the bank of the River Avon at West Amesbury.

From the entrance of the Stonehenge earthwork it follows the line of the axis, running past the Heel Stone to cross the main road, and continuing downhill for about a third of a mile, to the bottom of a dry valley. Its line can be traced by the growth of ranker grass and thistles along the ditches. It then swings sharply to the east and climbs the opposite slope to pass between the two prominent beech-woods on the skyline. There it swings gradually south-eastwards behind the nearer wood and descends the long slope to the river, crossing the main road again a little to the west of the turning to West Amesbury.

The Avenue probably marks the route by which the bluestones were hauled up from the river to Stonehenge. There is nothing else exactly like it, but it may have been copied in part from the nearby Cursus and in part from the avenues of standing stones which form the approaches to Avebury and a few other stone circles in other parts of Britain.

Only the stretch of the Avenue nearest to Stonehenge can now be made out on the ground. The rest of its course has long since been obliterated by cultivation, and was only re-discovered by air photography in 1923.

Above: *In the outer circle the sides of the lintels are cut to a curve.* Below: *On the trilithons the lintels have inclined sides, to correct the effects of perspective*

Above left: *The grooved bluestone in the Stonehenge horseshoe*. Above right:
*Rippled tooling on the side of a sarsen*. Below left: *The trilithon lintels are curved*.
Below right: *A battered tenon on a bluestone pillar*

# The Cursus

This extraordinary earthworks lies about half a mile (0.8 km) north of Stonehenge. It consists of a narrow enclosure, a mile and three-quarters (2.8 km) in length and a hundred yards (90 m) in width, bounded on either side by a low bank and ditch, like those of the Avenue. Just beyond its east end are the remains of a Long Barrow, on which the Cursus was evidently aligned. Most of its course has now been obliterated by ploughing, and there is little to be seen on the ground.

More than a dozen similar earthworks are known elsewhere in Britain, the longest of which extends for six miles (10 km). Their purpose is entirely unknown, but the most likely explanation is that they were processional ways used in some religious ceremony and perhaps connected with the cult of the dead, since a number of them are associated with Long Barrows and similar burial-places. They seem to belong to the Late Neolithic period, and the Stonehenge example was probably built at much the same time as the first monument at Stonehenge itself.

# Woodhenge

Woodhenge lies about two miles (3.2 km) north-east of Stonehenge, by the side of the main road from Amesbury to Marlborough (A345). It was discovered by air photography and excavated in 1928.

The outer boundary of the site consisted of a large circular bank, now almost flattened by ploughing, with a steep-sided flat-bottomed ditch inside it, about 6 ft (2 m) deep. The earthwork was broken by a single entrance-causeway on the north-north-east side.

Within the ditch the excavators found six concentric rings of circular holes for wooden posts, whose rotted stumps still survived in many cases. Their positions are now marked by concrete blocks, which give some idea of the original diameters of the posts.

Since nothing survived above ground, we can only guess what the remains represent. The most sensible explanation is that the posts formed the upright framework of a roofed building, like a huge barn bent round upon itself into a circle, leaving a space open to the sky in the centre.

The settings of posts are oval in plan, and the long axis of these ovals points in the direction of the midsummer sunrise, like the axis of Stonehenge. But the entrance here is not on the same line, and corresponds with the gap in the earthwork. This may mean that the earthwork was built first and the building within it added at a later date.

The plan of Woodhenge (opposite) *shows the rings of post-holes which the excavators found inside the remains of the earthwork. The larger holes have ramps running into them, to make it easier to erect the posts. How the posts were used is merely guess-work, but they make sense best as the framework of a circular building. The thickest and highest timbers would support the ridge of the roof, while the eaves would rest on thinner and shorter posts on the inside and outside, leaving an open light-well in the centre. A reconstructed elevation of the building is shown above the plan on the right*

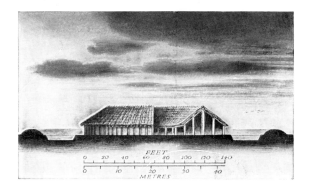

FEET
0    20    40    60    80    100    120    140
0        10        20        30        40
METRES

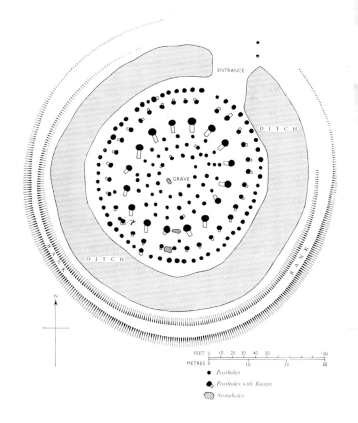

ENTRANCE

DITCH

GRAVE

DITCH

BANK

N

FEET 0 10 20 30 40 50        100
METRES 0            10            20            30

● Postholes

◐ Postholes with Ramps

▨ Stoneholes

On the axis, to the south-west of the centre, the excavators found a grave (now marked by a small cairn of flints) containing the body of a child about three years old, whose skull had been split before burial. This was evidently a dedicatory deposit, and is one of the very few pieces of evidence for human sacrifice in prehistoric Britain. South of this burial, in the second ring from the outside, there was a hole for an upright stone, now marked by an oblong block of concrete.

Scraps of pottery and other objects found during the excavations show that Woodhenge was built by the Secondary Neolithic people, who seem also to have been responsible for Stonehenge I. Since little or no domestic rubbish was found, it was clearly not a house; but beyond this we can only guess at its purpose. The most probable explanation is that it was a temple or place of public meeting.

# The Barrows

The region immediately round Stonehenge contains more prehistoric barrow-burials than any other area of the same size in Britain, and this concentration, like the grouping of graves round a church, must reflect the great sanctity of the district from Neolithic times onwards.

Many of the barrows are grouped in cemeteries, often strung out in a straight line. The most striking of these cemeteries lie on Normanton Down, on the skyline about half a mile (0·8 km) south of Stonehenge; and just north of the Winterbourne Stoke roundabout, which is a mile and a half (2·4 km) south-west of Stonehenge on the main road to Exeter (A303).

These cemeteries evidently cover a long period of time, during which changes took place in the shape of the barrows and the ritual of burial. The earliest type is the *Long Barrow*, the burial-place of the Primary Neolithic people. These were long mounds of chalk rubble quarried from a ditch on either side, covering at one end a number of bodies buried at the same time. There is a particularly fine example at the south end of the Winterbourne Stoke group, nearest the roundabout.

Most of the burials in these cemeteries are in *bowl barrows*, simple circular mounds, sometimes with a ditch immediately outside the edge of the mound. This type of burial, for a single person only, was introduced by the Beaker people and continued in use throughout the Bronze Age. In addition there are examples of two much rarer kinds of barrow, both of which seem to have been used by the Wessex people of the Early Bronze Age, the builders of Stonehenge III. *Bell barrows* have large mounds separated from the surrounding ditch by a flat platform, and sometimes a bank outside the ditch as well. They usually contain the burials of men,

*The buried ditches of the Stonehenge Avenue show up as lines of darker growth in the crops. The two beech woods on the right can be seen from Stonehenge on the eastern skyline*

sometimes accompanied by weapons and ornaments which suggest that they were warrior-chieftains. There is a fine example a short distance east of Stonehenge, close to the main road to Amesbury.

*Disc barrows*, on the other hand, are almost always women's graves. They consist of a flat circular area bounded by a ditch with a bank outside it, only a small tump at the centre marking the actual burial. Good examples can be seen in the Winterbourne Stoke group and on the crest of Normanton Down on either side of the track leading from Stonehenge.

*This prehistoric cemetery, a mile and a half south-west of Stoneheng*

*cludes a Long Barrow as well as Bowl, Bell and Disc Barrows*

# Avebury

The great earthwork and stone circles of Avebury, lying among the elm
trees on the edge of the water-meadows of the Kennet valley, form the
centre of a unique group of early prehistoric monuments in north Wiltshire, just as on Salisbury Plain a similar group clusters round Stonehenge.
Yet, in spite of its far greater size, Avebury has never attracted as much
notice as Stonehenge. The first account of it dates only from a visit made by
the antiquary John Aubrey in 1646; and it was hardly known at all to the
general public until 1743, when William Stukeley published his book *Abury*.
Since then excavations have been carried out here and on other neighbouring sites at various times, culminating in the extensive restoration of
half of Avebury by the late Mr Alexander Keiller from 1934 to 1939.
During this work a number of buried stones were found, which were set up
in their original positions; and the sites of other stones which had vanished
were marked with concrete blocks.

The main features of Avebury are the great surrounding earthwork and
the various settings of great stones which it encloses. The earthwork consists of a roughly circular ditch, originally cut with steep sides and a flat
bottom, which is now everywhere silted up to at least half its former depth.
The chalk rubble dug out of the ditch was piled in a great bank on its outer
side, and was originally separated from the ditch by a flat shelf or platform
about 15 ft (4·6 m) wide. The inner edge of the bank was retained by
a rough wall of chalk blocks, which has long since decayed.

There are four entrances through the earthwork, where the modern
roads now run. Three of these are known to be original features, and the
fourth, on the east side, is almost certainly an original entrance as well,
though it has not yet been tested by excavation.

Just within the inner lip of the ditch stand the remains of the Great
Circle of upright stones of which there were about 100 originally. Many
of them are very large, and the heaviest weigh over 40 tons. All of them,
and all the other stones at Avebury, are natural blocks of sarsen stone
hauled from the neighbouring downs; and unlike the stones of Stonehenge
they have not been dressed to shape. It seems likely, however, that the
builders deliberately selected the stones for their shape, since they are
mostly of two forms, a tall pillar with vertical sides and a broad diamond

*Avebury as it was in prehistoric times.*
*Compare this with the view today on the pages overleaf*

or lozenge, standing on one corner. The largest stones were placed flanking the entrances. Two of them survive at the south entrance, and the huge stone by the side of the Swindon road at the north entrance is doubtless the survivor of another pair.

Within the great circle are the remains of several smaller settings of stones. The *Central Circle* was originally about 320 ft (98 m) in diameter, and contained 30 stones of which only four now survive. At its centre was the *Cove*, consisting of three huge stones arranged on three sides of a square. Only two of them are now standing. Similar coves, whose purpose is likewise unknown, are associated with other stone circles at Stanton Drew in Somerset and Arbor Low in Derbyshire.

The *South Circle* was slightly larger, and contained 32 stones. Five of these survive, and the positions of four more are marked with concrete pillars. At the centre was a huge upright, 21 ft (6·4 m) long, which was still visible, though fallen, in the eighteenth century. To the west of the centre was a curious arrangement of smaller stones (known for convenience as the *Z Stones*), forming a straight line with extra stones set back from its ends; while outside the circle to the south, between it and the ditch, the excavators found the stump of an isolated stone, called the *Ring Stone* which until its destruction in the eighteenth century was perforated by a natural hole.

Just to the west of the northern entrance of the earthwork, the excavations revealed the holes for three stones, now marked with concrete, which obviously did not belong to the Great Circle. These were formerly believed to be the remains of a 'North Circle', of roughly the same size as the other two. But excavation of a wide arc of this circle has revealed no trace of any further holes, and it now seems certain that this northern circle never existed, or at any rate that no more than three of its stones were ever erected. In any case they must have been dismantled before the Great Circle was built.

Leading away from the south entrance of Avebury, the visitor will see the stones of the *Kennet Avenue*, which originally ran for about a mile southwards, passing the village of West Kennet and ending at the Sanctuary on Overton Hill. The northern third of the Avenue was excavated before the recent war, and the positions of the missing stones were marked in concrete. On the rest of its course very few stones are now visible.

The junction of the Avenue with the earthwork is awkwardly arranged, and looks like an afterthought on the part of the builders; and there is other evidence for a change in plan. Most of the stones in the central part of Avebury, and in the main part of the Avenue, are packed round their bases with small boulders and with clay brought from the banks of the Kennet near by; but there are a number of stone-holes also in which the packing-blocks are of hard chalk. This can have come only from the

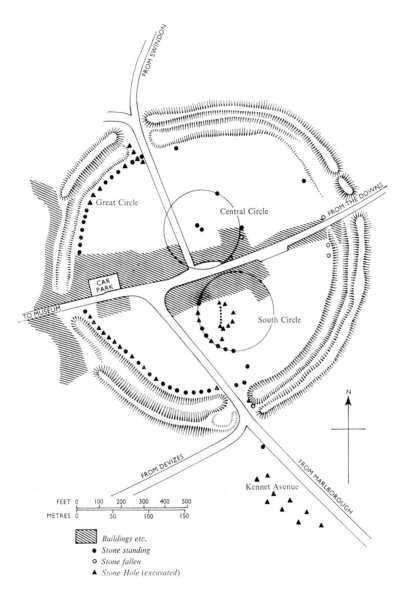

FROM SWINDON

Great Circle

Central Circle

FROM THE DOWNS

CAR PARK

TO MUSEUM

South Circle

N

FROM DEVIZES

FROM MARLBOROUGH

Kennet Avenue

FEET 0 100 200 300 400 500
METRES 0 50 100 150

Buildings etc.
● Stone standing
○ Stone fallen
▲ Stone Hole (excavated)

*Plan of the **Avebury** circles and the Kennet Avenue*

Above: *The stones of the Kennet Avenue, looking towards Avebury.* Below: *The south-west side of the Avebury earthwork and the Great Circle, seen from the south entrance*

bottom of the great ditch. On this evidence the building of Avebury can be divided into two periods.

*Avebury I* consisted of the Central and Southern Circles, together with the main part of the Avenue, which stopped short of the circles and did not point directly towards them. In the reconstruction which forms *Avebury II* the two circles were surrounded by the bank and ditch, with the Great Circle on its inner edge. At the same time the Ring Stone and the Z Stones were erected near the South Circle, and the former end of the Avenue was joined to the south entrance of the earthwork by additional stones forming a sharp bend.

Both these phases of building were probably the work of the Beaker people of the late Neolithic period, and can be dated between 2000 and 1600 BC. Two of their graves have been found at the feet of stones in the Avenue, and many broken scraps of their pottery lay in the excavated parts of the monument.

There has been far more destruction of the stones at Avebury than at Stonehenge, and as early as the fourteenth century a man, apparently a barber-surgeon, was trapped and killed by the sudden fall of a stone which he was helping to demolish. Most of the wrecking was done in the eighteenth century, to clear the ground for cultivation; and William Stukeley has left us a striking account of how the stones were tipped over a pit filled with burning straw and then smashed to pieces with sledge-hammers.

Above: *Part of the Great Circle at Avebury after its restoration.* Below: *Breaking up the Avebury stones in the 18th century with fire and sledge-hammers, to clear the ground for ploughing*

An Abury alto 20 f°. May 20. 1724

# West Kennet Long Barrow

This chambered tomb, the largest in England and Wales, lies about half a mile (0·8 km) south-west of the village of West Kennet. It is reached on foot from the Bath road along a path marked by a finger-post.

The barrow was considerably damaged in the seventeenth century, and was partially excavated in 1859. The excavation was completed and the tomb restored by the Ministry of Works (now the Department of the Environment) in 1955–57.

The mound is one of the largest known, measuring 350 ft (107 m) in length. It is made of chalk rubble dug out from a ditch on either side, now entirely silted up, piled over a core of sarsen boulders collected from the surface of the surrounding downs. The edge of the mound was originally marked, round the sides and back, by a line of boulders on end, but these have now all disappeared.

The front of the mound at the east end is formed by a façade of large upright stones, with the spaces between them filled with walling of stones brought from seven or eight miles away to the west. In the centre of the façade is a semi-circular forecourt, set back into the mound and bordered by four large slabs set on edge, out of which the tomb chamber opens.

The tomb itself consists of a long passage with two pairs of burial chambers opening off its sides and a larger chamber at the far end. The remains of about thirty skeletons, including ten children, were found on the floors of these chambers, and it is clear that they had been put in the tomb at intervals over a long period of time, the earlier deposits being swept unceremoniously aside to make room for new-comers. A good many bones, and especially skulls, seem to have been taken away while the tomb was still in use.

Pottery vessels deposited with some of these burials show that the tomb was used, though perhaps not built, by the Primary Neolithic people. It was probably constructed about 2700 BC, and continued to be used for many centuries.

After the last burial had been made, the whole tomb was blocked up in the most elaborate way. The chambers and passage were filled to the roof with chalk rubble containing numerous fragments of broken pottery and animal bones; and when this had been done the entrance-forecourt was first partially filled with boulders and then sealed off with three huge upright stones in line with those of the façade on either side, the centre stone being supported at the back by two uprights which continue the line of the passage. This final blocking seems to have been carried out by the local communities of Secondary Neolithic and Beaker people, who also built Avebury and the Sanctuary.

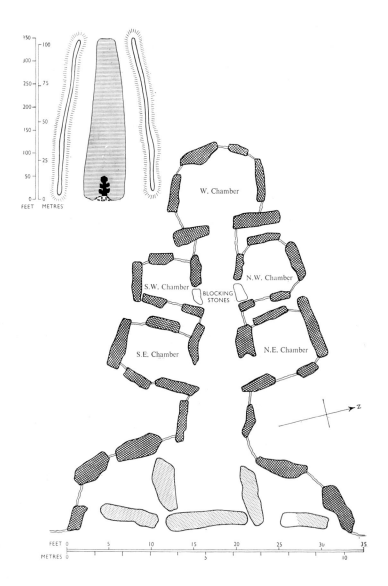

W. Chamber

S.W. Chamber

N.W. Chamber

BLOCKING
STONES

S.E. Chamber

N.E. Chamber

z

FEET 0    5    10    15    20    25    30    35
METRES 0         5              10

Left: *Plan of the West Kennet Long Barrow*
Above: *Neolithic burials in one of the chambers*
Below: *Offerings being made to the dead in front of the tomb*

# The Sanctuary

The Sanctuary lies on the south edge of the Bath road (A4) on the crest of Overton Hill, four and a half miles (7·2 km) west of Marlborough. Excavations carried out in 1930, in order to search for the remains of a stone circle which stood here until early in the nineteenth century, also revealed an earlier series of holes for wooden posts. The stone- and post-holes are now marked by concrete blocks and a coloured plan is displayed on a pillar on the south side.

Unlike Woodhenge, where the posts all seem to belong to a single building, the six rings of timbers here probably represent three separate structures built one after the other. The earliest was probably the ring of eight slender posts at the centre, standing as a sacred circle open to the sky. They may well have been carved and painted, like the sacred circles of the Indians of Virginia in the sixteenth century. The central post may belong with the others, or it may have been used as a centre-point for marking out one of the later buildings.

When the original circle was beginning to show signs of decay, an attempt seems to have been made to protect it by enclosing it in a circular building, whose roof was carried on two new rings of posts (Phase 2). This must have stood for some time, perhaps a couple of generations, as almost all the posts have been replaced as they decayed or became unsafe.

This building in turn was superseded by a larger one, which may also have been open at the centre to admit light and air. This is represented by the first and second ring from the outside, and the central ring of six larger posts (Phase 3). All these structures seem to have been the work of the local Secondary Neolithic population, who also built Woodhenge. They are probably earlier than any of the stone circles at Avebury.

Finally the site seems to have been taken over by the Beaker people, the builders of Avebury, who demolished the third wooden building and erected in its place two concentric circles of sarsen stones (Phase 4). This was probably done at the same time as the building of the Kennet Avenue, which leads up to and ends at the Sanctuary.

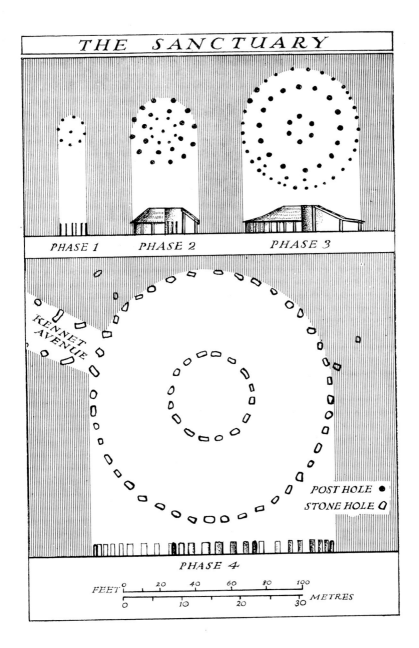

# THE SANCTUARY

PHASE 1    PHASE 2    PHASE 3

KENNET AVENUE

POST HOLE ●
STONE HOLE ▢

PHASE 4

FEET 0  20  40  60  80  100

METRES 0  10  20  30

# Silbury Hill

Silbury Hill, the largest artificial mound of antiquity in Europe, stands beside the Bath road (A4) about 6 miles (10 km) west of Marlborough.

The conical mound is 130 ft (40 m) high and covers 5½ acres (2·2 ha) at its base. The top is flat, and a short distance below it the side is broken by a marked terrace, now known to be an original feature. The surrounding ditch was originally about 125 ft (38 m) wide and 30 ft (9 m) deep, with a large extension towards the west. It is now almost completely filled with water-borne silt, as the result of long-continued flooding, except for the detached portion on the south side.

Excavations in 1968–69 showed that Silbury was built in three stages. *Silbury I* consisted of a central heap of gravelly clay capped by a turf stack within a ring of stakes, covered by layers of mixed materials derived from the flood-plain of the neighbouring stream. This was overlaid immediately by *Silbury II*, a very large mound of chalk excavated from a surrounding ditch. Before this was completed, however, the builders changed their minds in favour of an even larger mound. A new ditch was started further out, whose silted outlines can still be seen. The earlier ditch was filled up, and the chalk mound extended (*Silbury III*) so as to cover it completely. All this work, requiring the labour of at least 500 men for 10 years, took place about 2100 BC.

The construction of the mound shows an almost obsessive concern for stability. The piled material has been laid in horizontal layers, each divided into numerous sectors by radial and circumferential walls of chalk blocks; and the inner side of the ditch has been protected from frost-weathering, which would have undermined the edge of the mound, by piling against it horizontal layers of chalk rubble, held in place by timber revetment. These are features unknown elsewhere in earthworks of this early date, and they show that the builders of Silbury had a remarkable empirical knowledge of civil engineering, which they applied so effectively that the shape of the mound has hardly changed at all since it was built.

The purpose of Silbury remains a mystery, which the recent excavations have done no more to solve than did the investigations of the eighteenth and nineteenth centuries. If it is a burial mound (and this is still the most likely explanation), the burial itself must lie outside the central area which has been explored without result.

The turf stack at the centre preserves the prehistoric vegetation and insect life in remarkably good condition, and has allowed for the first time a detailed picture to be built up of the landscape, already much altered by man, in which Silbury, Stonehenge and other leading sites in the area were built.

Above: *The building of Silbury Hill.* Below: *Silbury Hill seen from the air. The ditch is now almost silted up, and water stands in it in winter*

# Windmill Hill

Windmill Hill is a dome-shaped chalk knoll which rises out of the Kennet valley a mile and a half (2·4 km) north-west of Avebury. It can be approached on foot, either from the main Swindon road (A361) a mile (1·6 km) north of Avebury, or by a track leading northwards from Avebury Trusloe.

The top of the hill is crowned by three concentric lines of earthworks forming a 'causewayed camp', so called because the ditches are interrupted by numerous gaps. The site was extensively excavated in the 1920s and has given its name to the Windmill Hill people, an early community of Neolithic farmers, who colonised southern England from the Continent about 3000 BC, and settled on the hill top soon afterwards. The earthwork enclosure, much of which has now been destroyed by ploughing, was built about 2500 BC. Its purpose is uncertain. The most probable explanation is that it was used as a ceremonial meeting-place for the local population, and perhaps as a tribal centre. The gaps in the ditches cannot all have been entrances, and are probably the result of splitting up the work of digging amongst a number of separate gangs. The banks inside the ditches were probably continuous originally, apart from one or two entrances, and may have been topped by fences or hedges of thorn.

No trace of houses or any permanent settlement was found inside the earthworks; but it must be remembered that since Neolithic times about 2 ft (600 mm) of chalk has been removed from the surface by weathering. In the ditches, the excavators found numerous deposits of wood ashes. broken pottery and animal bones, which had been carefully buried. These may well be the remains of ceremonial feasts. Some of the broken pottery must have been made as far away as Devon and Cornwall, showing that occasionally at least people travelled long distances to Windmill Hill.

Meetings of some kind seem to have taken place as late as 1500 BC, long after the earthwork enclosure had become denuded and silted up; and during the Bronze Age a number of barrows were built on the hill top.

*The many objects found in the excavation of Windmill Hill, Silbury Hill, Avebury and the Kennet Avenue are displayed in the Avebury Museum, which is reached through the churchyard. The finds from the Sanctuary and the West Kennet Long Barrow are in the Museum of the Wiltshire Archaeological Society, Long Street, Devizes.*

*Windmill Hill seen from the air. Only the excavated parts of the ditches show up clearly, but all three actually run right round the hill top*

# How were the monuments built?

The prehistoric monuments described in this guide are some of the finest and largest of their kind in Britain, and must be counted among the outstanding achievements of primitive engineering in Europe. But unfortunately we know very little about the methods used in their construction, and for the most part we have to rely on guess work aided by common sense.

The earthworks, large and small, all seem to have been built with the simplest tools. The chalk was loosened with 'picks' made from the antlers of red deer, many of which have been found abandoned on the bottoms of ditches. They were used, not like a modern pick, but as a handled wedge, the point of the 'pick' being driven into the soft rock by blows from a hammer on the back of the handle, which was then levered up to break away the chalk in fragments. Simple rakes, again made from antlers, were used to collect the rubble into heaps, which were then piled into baskets with small shovels made from the shoulder-blades of oxen. The loaded baskets were probably carried on the head, as they still are in many parts of the world; and in the deeper excavations ladders made of notched tree-trunks were doubtless used.

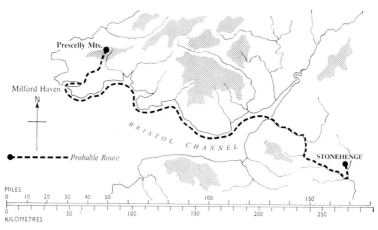

*The bluestones were probably carried on rafts from Wales*

56

Modern experiments with copies of these ancient tools have shown that two men, working in turns, can dig out about four cubic yards (3 cubic metres) of solid chalk in a day, and that from two to ten carriers would be needed for each pair of diggers, according to the depth of the ditch, to remove the rubble in baskets and dump it where required. At this rate it would have taken about two hundred people about nine years to build the earthwork at Avebury. To pile up Silbury Hill, nearly fifty million basketfuls of chalk, each weighing about 30 lb (14 kg), had to be carried up, or passed from hand to hand along a human chain, from the great ditch round its base.

The great posts used in the buildings at Woodhenge and the Sanctuary must all have been cut down and trimmed to shape with axes of flint and stone. Modern trials have shown that these tools, simple and crude though they look, are surprisingly efficient, and in the hands of skilled craftsmen can give results as good as modern tools of steel, though more slowly. On the stones of Stonehenge and the West Kennet Long Barrow there are a number of polished patches where stone tools have been sharpened by grinding during the course of the building work.

The transport and erection of the great stones must have been particularly difficult. The bluestones were probably brought from South Wales to Stonehenge mainly by water, loaded on rafts or boats. The most likely route runs from Milford Haven in Pembrokeshire along the south coast of Wales and up the Bristol Channel to Avonmouth; then up the Avon and Frome rivers to near Frome in Somerset, overland to near Warminster.

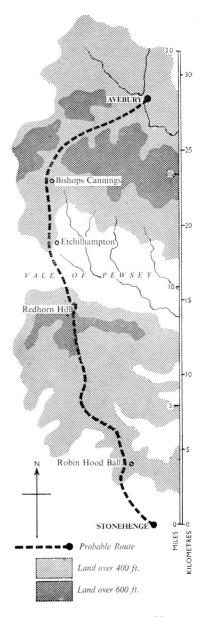

59

*The sarsen stones were hauled to Stonehenge from near Avebury on sledges and rollers. The best route follows the higher ground*

and thence by the Wylye and the Salisbury Avon to the end of the Stonehenge Avenue near West Amesbury. The total distance is about 240 miles (385 km).

In 1954 an experiment was made on the River Avon near Stonehenge, with the help of the BBC Television Service. A copy of a bluestone in concrete was loaded on to a composite boat, made of three copies of prehistoric dug-out canoes lashed together side by side. This vessel was poled up the river against the current by four schoolboys, and could have been handled by only one, if necessary. This kind of boat must certainly have been used for the inland part of the journey, because even when loaded its flat bottom was only 9 inches (230 mm) deep in the water; whereas a raft to carry much the same load would have been at least 2 ft. (600 mm.) deep, and would constantly have run aground in shallow places. But rafts were probably used at sea, because there is no danger of their sinking.

For the great sarsen stones used at Stonehenge and Avebury no suitable water route was available, and they must have been dragged overland all the way, probably mounted on rough sledges running on rollers, and hauled with ropes of leather or cow-hair. To bring the eighty-odd stones of Stonehenge more than twenty miles (32 km) from the Marlborough Downs may well have occupied a thousand men for several years.

In the same experiment in 1954, the copy of the bluestone, weighing 1½ tons, was loaded on a simple wooden sledge, and this could just be pulled up a gradient of about 1 in 14 (4°) by a party of 32 schoolboys. When the sledge was run on rollers, instead of directly on the grass, the size of the hauling party dropped to 14; and doubtless it could have been brought down to 10 if better and larger rollers had been available.

At this rate, the heaviest stone at Stonehenge, weighing about 50 tons, would have needed at least 100 men to pull it along on rollers on flat ground, and at least another 100 to lay the rollers in front of the sledge and keep it from wandering sideways. To pull the stone up the steepest slope likely to be encountered on the journey, with a gradient of 1 in 6½ (9°), would need at least an extra 350 men. The journey with a single stone from the Marlborough Downs to Stonehenge, and back again with the empty sledge and the rollers, must have taken at least two weeks.

The method of erecting the stones seems to have been the same in all cases. A foundation pit was dug, with one side vertical and the opposite one in the form of a sloping ramp. Stakes, stripped of their bark, were driven in against the vertical side to protect the chalk from being crushed by the toe of the stone as it was gradually raised. The stone, base foremost, was then moved on rollers towards the ramp, until its toe was over the hole, and its centre of gravity was just behind the leading roller (1). The outer end was then levered up, dipping the base into the hole, until the stone overbalanced at the last moment and came to rest in a leaning

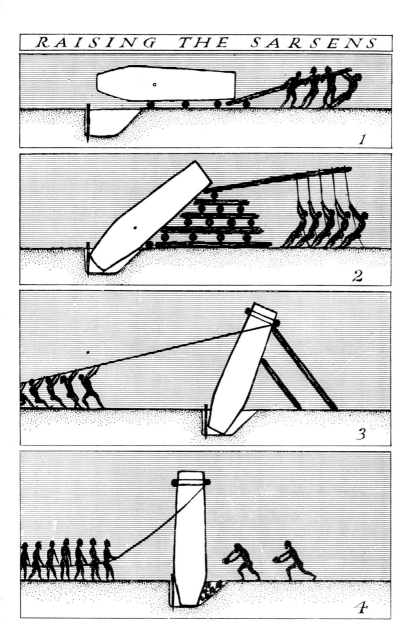

The lintels of Stonehenge were probably raised a foot or two at a time on stacked lengths of timber which surrounded the uprights and provided a working platform level with their tops.

position. Next, with levers resting on timber packing (2), it was raised a few inches at a time and held in place with struts when the packing had to be adjusted (3). Finally the stone would be pulled upright by gangs of men hauling on ropes (4). To raise a stone of the outer circle at Stonehenge would need about 200 men.

To help in adjusting the position of the stones, their bases were left in the form of a blunt point, on which the mass could pivot; and when the final adjustment had been made the hole was rapidly filled and rammed tight with whatever lay at hand including, at Stonehenge, many of the stone hammers previously used in dressing the surfaces of the stones.

The capstones of the tomb at West Kennet were probably hauled into position only when the surrounding mound had been piled up to the level of the tops of the walls, which would meantime have been strutted with timber. But at Stonehenge there was no mound, and here the lintels must have been raised gradually by means of levers and a crib. This is a kind of tower, built of alternate layers of timber running in opposite directions. The lintel would first be raised a foot or two on temporary supports. The lowest layers of the crib would then be laid around and beneath it, and planked over on top. The weight of the lintel would then be transferred with levers to this planking, and the whole process repeated until the stone was level with the tops of the uprights and could be levered sideways into position.

# HOURS OF ADMISSION

## STONEHENGE

|  | *Weekdays* | *Sundays* |
|---|---|---|
| March to April | 9.30 am to 5.30 pm | 9.30 am to 5.30 pm |
| May to September | 9.30 am to 7.00 pm | 9.30 am to 7.00 pm |
| October | 9.30 am to 5.30 pm | 2.00 pm to 5.30 pm |
| November to February | 10.00 am to 4.30 pm | 2.00 pm to 4.30 pm |

ADMISSION FEE: Adults: 10p   Children under 15: 5p

## AVEBURY MUSEUM

The hours of admission are the same as at Stonehenge.

Stonehenge is the property of the Department of the Environment. Avebury and Windmill Hill were placed in the guardianship of the Ministry of Public Building and Works (now the Department of the Environment) by the National Trust.

SEASON TICKETS, valid for a year from the date of issue, admit their holders to all ancient monuments and historic buildings in the care of the State. Tickets can be purchased at many monuments; at HMSO bookshops; and from the Department of the Environment (AMSS/P), Neville House, Page Street, London SW1, who will supply full information on request.

*Acknowledgment is made to Professor Stuart Piggott for the drawing on page 23; to Aerofilms Ltd for the pictures on pages 12 and 40–41 and the lower picture on page 53; to the Ashmolean Museum, Oxford, for those on pages 35 and 36–37; to the Bodleian Library, Oxford, for the lower picture on page 46; to the University of Cambridge for the picture on page 55; to the Department of Prehistoric Archaeology, University of Edinburgh, for the upper picture on page 49; and to Gateway Film Productions Ltd for the pictures on pages 19 and 20. The pictures on pages 4 and 5, the lower photograph on page 23, the lower picture on page 26, the pictures on pages 29 and 30, and the maps (redrawn) on pages 56 and 59 are from 'Stonehenge', by R. J. C. Atkinson (Hamish Hamilton, 1956), by permission of the publishers.*

Dd. 503558  K720  9/71          Printed in England for Her Majesty's Stationery Office
                                by Swindon Press, Swindon